A 3rd *Freedom*

2nd

1st

Brooks B. Robinson

Published by BlackEconomics.org, an Internet portal that
features analysis of Black economic concepts, issues,
policies and plans; Honolulu, Hawaii.

Dedication

To my mother, Delia, who lived through the first and
second freedoms.

Table of Contents

Introduction 1

The First Freedom 5

   Introduction 5

   Settling the slaves 7

   Acquiring land in the south 9

   Independent living arrangements 12

   Conclusion 13

The Second Freedom 15

   Introduction 15

   Winning legal and legislative victories 16

   Integrating unequal entities 18

   Rolling back the second freedoms 21

   Conclusion 26

A Third Freedom 28

   Introduction 28

   Who told you that you were naked? 29

   What do African descendants want? 32

   Reparations 36

   A Homeland 38

   PAPS (Prayers answered and problems solved) 40

   Old wine into new skins 42

   Everlasting life 44

Epilogue 46

Index 48

Introduction

In a world of luck and chance, it is often said that "the third time is the charm." It is, therefore, fitting that US African descendants will find our third thrust for freedom to be the one that makes us free indeed. No doubt a great deal of effort went into our pursuit of the first two freedoms. However, given our lack of knowledge as strategic thinkers and planners at the time, it took lots of luck and prayers to wrest from an obstinate and hard taskmaster freedom from chattel slavery and access to civil rights. These first two freedoms, while beneficial in many respects, did not permit access to true liberty—*the ability to do what we want the way we want.* In fact, the first two freedoms created a false sense of liberty, which caused US African descendants to delay or slow the pace toward ultimate freedom.

After the Civil War and the onset of Reconstruction, US African descendants were lulled into believing that great accomplishments had been achieved, and that there would be irreversible change. The arising of the Ku Klux Klan helped contract the Reconstruction Era. Jim Crow laws followed and sharecropping systems that returned US African descendants to economic bondage that had many elements that were akin to chattel slavery—particularly in southern states. Despite these opposing forces, Robert Higgs revealed in 1982 that US African descendants worked, saved, and acquired more land in the State of Georgia than did European Americans during 1880 - 1910. This is not a well-known fact. It defies status quo thinking about the era. Nevertheless, US African descendants showed great resourcefulness in achieving this outcome.

World Wars I and II moved the US forward in finding ways to utilize "free" US African descendant labor. But after the wars, US African descendants awakened to the reality of severe political, social, educational, and economic inequality in the land, and we embarked upon the Civil Rights Movement. The 1954 *Brown v. Board of Education Topeka* Supreme Court Decision, the 1955 Montgomery Bus Boycott, the 1963 March on Washington, the Civil Rights Act of 1964, and the Fair Housing Act of 1968, were victory signposts that made US African descendants believe, once again, that freedoms had been squeezed out of European Americans' hands. The thirst and thrust for freedom continued until Martin Luther King, Jr. was assassinated in 1968, which started a trek down the back side of the mountain whose peak he envisioned. By the late 1970s, the *Bakke* Supreme Court Decision began to help reverse many Affirmative Action practices, and US African descendants realized that freedom, in its full form, had escaped us again.

Circa 1977, when we asked Kwame Ture (aka Stokely Carmichael) why the movement had halted, he explained that the halt was temporary. He said that the people were working on resolving ideological issues and that once the ideology was sorted out, then that would be the end of the ball game. That is, once US African descendants decided exactly what we wanted from the American system, then we would press our way to that conclusion without hesitation.

The 1980s brought Ronald Reagan and the "Me Generation," the "Hip Hop Generation," HIV AIDS, and a crack cocaine epidemic. The 1990s brought Generation X, the arising and proliferation of computer technology, and an explosion of the prison industrial complex that found US African descendant males as readily available subjects. The first decade of the 21st century took the nation to war against terrorism and, as before, US African descendants (male and female) joined in the fight as a way of keeping food on the table. However, the Great Recession of 2008-9 produced very high unemployment for African descendants and, even with the ongoing wars, African descendants lost vast ground on the economic front. The election of an African descendant president, Barack Obama, turned out to be a footnote and not a volume of change.

We are now in the second decade of the 21st century, and ideological issues appear to continue to change without much resolution. In 2013, 2014, and 2015, there was a new airing of police force brutality and shootings of US African descendant males, and significant organization around that issue. Yet, no force has arisen with power sufficient to capture the imagination of the US African descendant nation and turn it on a dime toward a long-term goal that will result in true liberty. Unfortunately, our HOPE, that "talented tenth," has not taken the time to converge to evolve a long-term strategic plan that will get us to true liberty.

For this nation of over 45 million US African descendants, the time is arriving for a thrust toward *A 3rd Freedom*. This monograph revisits the first two freedoms, then points us toward that third freedom. It is our very strong belief that, if we do not arise and challenge for the third freedom, then another outcome will be imposed upon us and it is not likely to be a preferred outcome. Unfortunately, there are likely to be several distractions that contrive to turn us away from freedom. If we are to succeed, then we must remain resolute and convinced that it is our right to enjoy true liberty just as do people of nations the world over.

The goal has never been to just be free from slavery, to just extricate ourselves from Jim Crow, to just be able to live peaceably in homes next to European Americans and to go to school with them, or just to experience a semblance of income or even wealth equality. No, the goal has always been to experience complete freedom; i.e., *to do what we*

3

want the way we want. Inherently, we have always known that that can only occur when we live in a nation of our own.

The First Freedom

Introduction

The Emancipation Proclamation of 1863 and the subsequent conclusion of the Civil War in 1865 marked the "first freedom" for US African descendants. So much has already been written concerning this period that it is difficult to contribute to the literature and not be redundant. Which niche do we plan to fill? We want to scour the landscape and identify evidence concerning African descendants' recognition that they were, in fact, experiencing a first freedom. That is, we plan to convey information that indicates incomplete pleasure with history as it unfolded, and a displeasure that more was not obtained. This is best seen not by African descendants' rush to interact with European Americans in order to show the former's equality with the latter, but by African descendants' thirst for land and a place that they could call their own.

At the end of the Civil War, there must have been a dearth of communication up and down the geographical and economic African descendant hierarchy. Consequently, one could not logically raise the question of unification of the total African descendant population in the United States. Without this essential unification element it was not possible to raise a strong voice for nation formation within US borders. History tells us that there had been, over the course of time, several plans to relocate African descendants to distant territories. In fact, there had also been small suggestions that African descendants be transplanted in the Northwest Territory. But for a variety of reasons none of these proposals came to fruition.

In the absence of a solid plan for nation formation, what we find is individual African descendants working extremely hard to secure resources to purchase a plot of land that they could call their own. In addition, where possible, and where small groups of African descendants (extended families and groups of former slaves from common plantations or communities) could agree, they forged bonds and squeezed out land for themselves and established independent living arrangements for themselves. This signifies that they understood, even then, that they would never be accepted fully by Europeans, and that they sought to live on their own so that they could determine their own life path. In every way, this is a story about a people who gained a freedom, but who understood that it was not the ultimate freedom to which they aspired. The implication is that they lived and survived in order that their posterity would realize a more favorable future freedom.

Due to the lack of communication, there was an absence of goal specification. What was the ultimate goal of the freed slaves? Even down to today, ask African descendants what our ultimate goal(s) is(are), and you will receive a response of "I don't know" or a list of aspirations that can only be considered interim in nature—not ultimate. Therefore, we intend to look for evidence that African descendants really did not understand what their ultimate goal was following the Civil War and in the years thereafter.

In reality, African descendants' actions following the Civil War should inform our actions today. In considering their action in this section of this monograph, we revisit history's recording of plans to dispense with former slaves. We hear pro and con voices on resettlement in and outside of US borders. We explore a very important finding concerning the extent to which, and the rate at which, African descendants acquired land in the early post-bellum period. We take note of the numerous independent living arrangements that highlighted African descendants' desire to live with each other and away from European Americans. All of this we do with the hope of unearthing a better understanding concerning African descendants' perspective about the future. We believe that they knew that more than this first freedom was to come—and had to come—if they expected to achieve fulfillment on America's shores.

Settling the slaves

In 1820, the American Colonization Society (ACS) formed and emphasized for decades alternating weak and intense thrusts to relocate former slaves and freedmen to Africa's western coast. However, the expense and distance associated with this effort, in addition to the economics and politics of the matter, meant that it could only experience limited success. Nevertheless, the records show that nearly 11 thousand African descendants had been transported back to Africa by the time the Civil War got underway in 1860.[1]

Lusane (2011) takes considerable space in *The Black History of the White House* to highlight plans concerning what to do with Negro slaves leading up to and during the Civil War, which was the topic of many conversations in the White House.[2] It is clear that President Abraham Lincoln's preference was for African descendants to emigrate either back to Africa or to Central America (viz., the Chiriqui Plan), which was based on rather racist principles. At the same time, Lusane argues that those African descendants who advocated for leaving the US did so as an expression of "self-determination, racial solidarity, and genuine democratic aspirations" (p. 188). In the end, it turns out that

---

[1]See Table 2 in Eric Burin (2005), *Slavery and the Peculiar Solution: A History of the American Colonization Society*, University Press of Florida, Gainesville, Florida.
[2] Clarence Lusane (2011), *The Black History of the White House*, City Lights Books, San Francisco, California.

many African descendants who knew about the choice and who had an opportunity to voice an opinion about it rejected Lincoln's idea of emigration just as they had rejected ACS efforts to populate the Liberia Colony. The reality is that many African descendants who rejected emigration were educated, or at least literate, and mostly resided in the northern portion of the country. There is no such clear view concerning the opinions of the millions of Black slaves who were in the south; they are not likely to have known about the choice, and definitely did not have an opportunity to express their opinions about it.

Article six of the Northwest Ordinance of 1787 made slavery illegal in the Northwest Territory. Therefore, it was considered a possible location, by some, for settlement of former slaves. In addition, the Homestead Act of 1862, which opened western territories to settlement at relatively cheap prices, became relevant for freed slaves as a potential source of land to build a life. However, much of the most favorable land was already claimed by the time these slaves were eligible to exercise their right following the Emancipation Proclamation and the conclusion of the Civil War. Moreover, most slaves were absent financial resources to travel to a new homestead and fulfill requirements for homesteading. Nevertheless a considerable number of African descendants made their way west following the first freedom. Expression of their desire to experience self-determination is most obvious in the numerous Black towns that sprouted throughout the western frontier. Taylor (1998) reports that 32 all-Black towns came to exist in Oklahoma and the Indian Territory following the Civil War.[3] He goes on to cite historian Kenneth Hamilton who identified 46

---

[3] Quintard Taylor (1998), *In Search of the Racial Frontier: African Americans in the American West 1528-1990*, W.W. Norton & Company, New York, New York.

Black towns in five western states in the late 19th century (p.148).

All of this tells us that many well-to-do African descendants rejected President Lincoln's idea of self-determination on an emigration basis. However, African descendants of more moderate means who were able to go west in the second half of the 19th century did so with the intent of finding a way to establish independent (of European Americans) living arrangements. They may or may not have known about the potential prospect of establishing a free and independent nation outside of the US, but they certainly expressed an intent to be as independent of European Americans as they could possibly be while still residing in the US. These independent living arrangements lay far from well-developed areas in the eastern and southern parts of the country, and the former reflected little connection with the latter. Consequently, it is reasonable to argue that those African descendants who moved west, especially those who lived in all-Black towns, would have expressed a preference for nation formation for African descendants—given an opportunity to do so.

Acquiring land in the South

Those African descendants who remained behind in the South following the Civil War also expressed a strong interest in being independent. We see this expression in the extent to which, and the rate at which, these African descendants acquired real estate for farming and other purposes. The great Black scholar W.E.B. DuBois wrote extensively on this issue. However, we use as our primary source here the work of Robert Higgs (1982) to construct our arguments; he builds on DuBois work and cites many of them.[4]

Using mainly statistical (specifically econometric) analysis, Higgs derives several important conclusions. First, he shows that, in the post-bellum period up to 1910, African descendants reduced the wealth gap with European Americans by half: from European Americans having 32 times more wealth than African descendants in 1880, to European Americans having just 16 times more wealth than African descendants in 1910. The data and the analysis concerns the state of Georgia. However, the nature of Georgia as a former slave state should lead us to believe that similar developments were occurring all over the South. This outcome signals that African descendants were intent on carving out a life for themselves in this former hell. They were not satisfied to sit idly by and watch the world go past. No, they wanted to do for themselves and they did.

Second, Higgs (1982) shows that, throughout the post-bellum period up to 1910, the percentage of African descendants' wealth that was associated with farm real estate was always higher than the percentage of wealth that was associated with urban real estate. In our view, this sends a variety of signals including the fact that, all else being equal, there was a preference for generating a living arrangement that allowed one to be independent and away from very close contact and interaction with European Americans, which would have occurred in urban areas.

Third, Higgs (1982) shows that the growth of literacy among African descendants was an important and positive factor that contributed to the growth of their wealth. The evidence

---

[4] Robert Higgs (1982), "Accumulation of Property by Southern Blacks before World War I," *American Economic Review*, Vol. 72, No. 4; pp. 725-37.

is that African descendants were able to secure and maintain their wealth the greater was the extent of their literacy—the ability to read and comprehend legal documents. In other words, their thirst for knowledge was fueled partly by a desire to protect themselves from European Americans who developed a proclivity to steal wealth from African descendants who were illiterate. This latter condition logically implies another reason why African descendants wanted to establish independent living arrangements away from European Americans.

The rate of wealth accumulation by African descendants in the post-bellum period makes clear their intent to operate independent lives. The fact that they concentrated more on farms, while consistent with their human capital in agriculture and buying power, also reflects an interest in forming the most independent (of European Americans) lifestyle possible. Finally, African descendants learned early on that their success in the new era hinged on their ability to read and write. Combined, these developments could not constitute a position or sense of finality for African descendants. It was clear that they remained in enemy territory—physically, socially, and economically. They had to work, struggle, and fight to build wealth in what remained an antagonistic and discriminatory environment. They must have known that there was a need for further developments and resolution of issues if their lives were to ever be peaceful. What were these developments and resolutions to be? Obviously, they did not know. History tells us that they trusted their God and bought time by taking it one day at a time—hoping that future generations would experience improved outcomes.

Independent living arrangements

Robinson (2011) explores three cases where African descendants established very successful and independent living arrangements: Wilmington, North Carolina; Tulsa, Oklahoma; and Rosewood, Florida.[5] These three locales featured numerous successful African descendant businesses and social institutions, and the populations were able to amass widespread wealth that was not present in most other locales where African descendants resided. For example, the area occupied by African descendants in Tulsa was known as "Black Wall Street." The Wilmington and Tulsa cases involved urban (city) settings, while Rosewood was a more rural (town-like) setting. Those who are familiar with the history of these locales know that, in the end, European Americans attacked violently African descendants for no legitimate reasons and murdered considerable numbers. In the case of Wilmington and Tulsa, European Americans also burned significant portions of the infrastructure that African descendants had constructed as part of their broader prosperity. These historical atrocities occurred in early 20th century; however, these centers of African descendant success began to form in the 19th century.

These three locales are testaments to two arguments that are aligned with our discussion of the "first freedom." First, as Higgs (1982) confirms, African descendants tended to be more successful economically the greater was their concentration in the population in the surrounding area. Contrary to the argument that many put forward today concerning African descendants' "inability to get along and govern themselves," the three locales cited here and the many all-Black towns discussed above, reflect the fact that

[5] See Brooks B. Robinson (2011), *53*, BlackEconomics.org, Honolulu, Hawaii.

African descendants could "get along and govern themselves." Importantly, African descendants understood each other's needs and produced goods and services to meet those needs, which permitted the circulation of their money among themselves that facilitated economic growth.

Second, these locales constitute an argument that African descendants wanted to live with each other and away from the conflicts that were associated with life with European Americans. While African descendants did not take action to establish a separate national territory during the post-bellum period, they certainly took action when and wherever possible to develop separate living spaces within the national territory. It is as if they were saying, "We can't leave this hell, but we certainly will make every effort to establish our own heaven in the confines of this hell." This attitude is, in our view, consistent with an unstated desire to form a nation. In fact, at this stage in US History, it may have only been the absence of a communications mechanism that prevented greater consolidation and integration among African descendants and a nation building effort.

Conclusion

No question about it, the first freedom, like many first-ever events, must have been particularly joyous. Yet it was fraught with concerns about how to survive and move forward. African descendants accepted the challenge and were successful both in departing former slave territory and in remaining in the former slave states following the Civil War. Importantly, many of those who went west formed all-Black towns. Those who remained behind in the south worked hard and acquired wealth, especially land, at a rate more rapid than that of European Americans. Much of this wealth was in the form of farms, which permitted African descendants the freedom to be independent. It is also true that, even in urban areas in the South, African descendants fashioned their own separate urban areas. While this outcome, on the surface, may appear to be politically, racially, and economically determined, the reality is that African descendants generally expressed an interest in living together—as opposed to desiring to integrate with European Americans. In fact, the data show that African descendants fared better economically the greater their concentration in the population.

All of this points us back to our conclusion that African descendants may not have had the wherewithal to develop an overarching long-term strategic plan due to the absence of communications and consolidation in the immediate post-bellum period. Nevertheless, they were successful in determining that it was in their best interest to stick and work together to survive and seek to grow as a people. Their expression of lifestyle independence as part of this first freedom is tantamount to saying:

> If we had an opportunity, then we would live separate and apart from European Americans. Barring that, we will live with and by ourselves, to the extent possible, with the hope that one day a true and more complete freedom can be achieved.

After much turmoil, a second freedom would come, which we explore in the next section.

The Second Freedom

Introduction

A second freedom had to come. The first freedom in the form of the Emancipation Proclamation and the Civil War, which freed Negro slaves, was insufficient to meet the aspirations of the new freedmen. They went about the business of exercising their freedoms to the extent possible. However, as you know, restraints were imposed on those freedoms. Freedoms were inhibited mainly by a Jim Crow system, which included Vagrancy Laws, that prevented African descendants from voting, and other measures that stifled ownership of property, moving freely within certain business establishments, and excluded African descendants from many educational institutions. The most notorious barrier to freedom was the right of African descendants and European Americans to interact freely together. Probably more than any other action, males of African descent would be lynched just for "looking" at European American females; viz., Emmitt Till. In fact, the enforcement by European Americans of laws that prevented African descendants from exercising the latter's freedom may be best exemplified by the fact that over 1,800 African descendants were lynched during the 20th century.[6]

In light of this reality, African descendants had to conjure up a second freedom. As was the case with the abolitionist movement, which helped motivate the end of slavery, African descendants had to advocate on their own behalf to stimulate systemic changes that would open the door to more

---

[6] This statistic is derived from data provided by the University of Missouri-Kansas City School of Law. Retrieved from the Internet on April 14, 2015; http://law2.umkc.edu/faculty/projects/ftrials/shipp/lynchingyear.html.

freedoms—freedoms that, in many cases, they were already entitled to legally.

In this section of the monograph, we discuss efforts by African descendants to motivate the second freedom, including the great legal and legislative victories that helped the second freedom unfold. However, we point out that the goal that was established as the *sine qua non* of the second freedom—desegregation/racial integration—was problematic from the outset. Consequently, it did not produce desired outcomes, and it faced opposition all along the way to rollback or to hamper the full exercise of the second freedom. In addition, we cannot discuss the second freedom without realizing that it, too, could not be viewed as an ultimate freedom. As a result, we see the second freedom as insufficient to address the aspirations of African descendants, and we anticipate a thrust for a third freedom.

Winning legal and legislative victories

Let us be frank, we can mark the onset of the second freedom with the 1954 *Brown vs. Board of Education of Topeka* US Supreme Court decision. The court simply said that separate was unequal, which set the stage for a push forward to the second freedom based on the concept of equality. It is noteworthy that, while the language focused on "equality," which had severe implications for European Americans, in reality, the focus was on "equal treatment." It is one thing to discuss a path to equality (in education, politics, and economics), it is another thing altogether just to say that one will be treated equally in these areas. In the former case, European Americans would have been forced to give up something; in the latter case, the implication is that African descendants would have an opportunity to be treated equally. The key point to remember is that, in either case, vast resources would have been required to enforce equality or equal treatment. The reality is that only limited resources were provided to enforce laws that were designed to guarantee equal treatment.

Then came the Montgomery Bus Boycott, Lunch Counter Sit-Ins, and Freedom Rides. These motive forces resulted in the 1963 March on Washington and ultimately in the 1964 Civil Rights Act. These seemingly positive pressures to produce a second freedom were followed by the Selma March in 1965 and the Fair Housing Act of 1968. Notably, in 1965, the concept of Affirmative Action was reinforced by President Lyndon Johnson's Executive Order 11246, and it appeared that the nation was on its way to equal treatment and integration, which might ultimately result in equality.[7]

But this was not to be because the method used to operationalize integration was, by design, guaranteed to fail from the very outset. When US governments at all levels began to integrate African descendant youth with European American youth in elementary and secondary schools and in colleges and universities, when African descendant families began to move into European American neighborhoods, when African descendant politicians began to compete with European American politicians, and when African descendant businesses began to compete with European American businesses, failure was the only possible outcome. Why? Because it is insane to think that a majority European American population should be expected to willingly relinquish their position of power. In addition, it is impossible to integrate two unequal entities and expect a balanced outcome. If one mixes black and white paint of unequal proportions (more white than black), you get a very light gray—almost white, not a rich dark gray.

---

[7] President Johnson reinforced Affirmative Action; the concept was first included in President John F. Kennedy's Executive Order 10925 in 1961, which was mainly an employment-based measure.

Integrating unequal entities

Our argument is that the African descendant leadership that was in place as the second freedom unfolded did not take the time to think through the implications of their decisions. They committed an error in strategy. Importantly, they did not have a long-term strategic plan—if they did, it was not sound. Therefore, the leadership opted for what sounded like a valid proposition, but, in fact, it was not. Let us explore the situation critically.

We must admit that when desegregation/racial integration began, African descendants comprised a very underdeveloped group, while European Americans comprised a very developed group. As Figure 1 shows, for all intents and purposes, the European American group was above (superior) to African descendants on an educational, political, and economic basis. The power that they possessed

Figure 1.—Actual US Desegregation/Integration Process

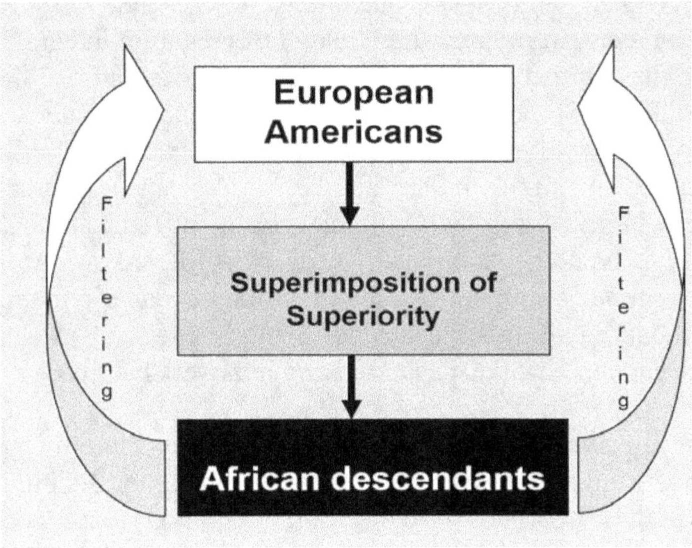

European
Americans

Filtering

Superimposition of
Superiority

Filtering

African descendants

Figure 2.—Ideal US Desegregation/Integration Process

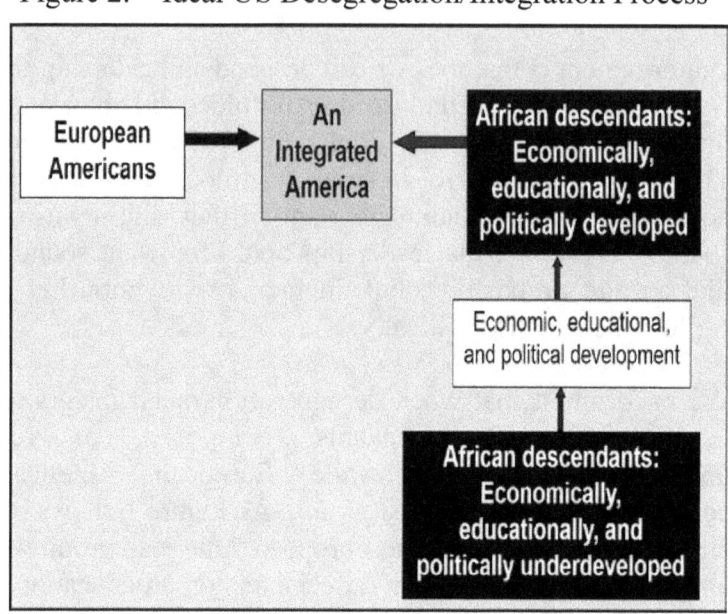

enabled European Americans to stand above African descendants and dictate outcomes. In the end, European Americans were pressured into desegregation/integration and they agreed to go along, but only to the extent that they could control the number of African descendants who were allowed to filter up and receive equal treatment. This resulted in only a limited number of African descendants receiving a certain level of equal treatment (educationally, politically, and economically) as the few filtered up. At the same time, the majority of African descendants remained without equal treatment, and a high levels of African descendants lived dispossessed and impoverished lives.

Conversely, Figure 2 characterizes an appropriate method for pursuing the desegregation/integration game. As Figure 2 shows, before desegregation/integration can occur between unequal entities and produce a balanced outcome, the entities must be brought into equality. In this case, the underdeveloped African descendant population should have obtained access to resources to develop (educationally, politically, and economically) separately first, which would have elevated us to a position of equality with European Americans, and then the two groups could have been desegregated/integrated to produce a balanced outcome. But even this scenario begs the question of what was the long-term goal of African descendants?

In the recently released movie "Selma," there are at least two telling points in this regard. First, the movie has Dr. Martin Luther King, Jr. asking his comrade, Dr. Ralph Abernathy, concerning the path that should be taken in the Civil Rights Movement. Abernathy's reply is that (paraphrasing) "we take it one step at a time, building the path brick-by-brick." Second, Dr. King tells Dr. Abernathy, (paraphrasing) "What does it matter that an African descendant can sit at a lunch counter with a European American if the former does not have the money to purchase a hamburger." In the first case, the path to take on such an important historical trek as the Civil Rights Movement should not be decided on a piecemeal basis ("brick-by-brick"); rather there should be great strategizing, placing the entire era in the context of an elongated historical period—definitely 100 years if not 500 years. In the second case, what was the meaning of desegregation/integration if African descendants could not compete? The playing field was not level. And even if African descendants had the money to purchase the hamburger, but could not compete with European Americans, then what was the real benefit? After 350 years of slavery and Jim Crow, did not African descendants want more out of America than just being able to say that they could go to the same bathroom with European Americans?

Therefore, from the very outset, the second freedom unfolded toward failure. No long-term goal was established to bring African descendants to an ultimate freedom that they could enjoy. In addition, the goal that was established, desegregation/integration, was operationalized improperly. Importantly, European American did not favor this path and began to find ways to thwart the effort in so many ways.

Rolling back the second freedoms

A sharp and critical look at history will reveal that European Americans took action at every turn to rollback, to the extent possible, all of the benefits that comprised the second freedom. Whether we are concerned with the 1978 *Regents of the University of California vs. Bakke* Supreme Court case, the onset of the Acquired Immune Deficiency Syndrome (AIDS) epidemic in the early 1980s, the crack cocaine epidemic of the 1980s and 1990s, the prodigious expansion of the prison industrial complex during the 1990s and the first decade of the 21st century, the dot.com era during the second half of the 1990s, or the financial and economic crisis of 2008/9 (the Great Recession), one can find evidence that African descendants were on the adverse side of the outcomes. Let us take a moment to consider each of these in turn.

As noted above, Affirmative Action had come out of the President Lyndon Johnson era, and was designed to open up opportunities for African descendants to receive equal treatment mainly in education, employment, and business opportunities. As it turned out, initially the number of African descendants who were being admitted to colleges and universities, particularly professional programs (such as medicine and law), expanded sharply during the early 1970s. Then came the *Bakke* case, which argued that Affirmative

Action was a case of "reverse discrimination." That is, by setting aside seats in professional schools for African descendants, educational institutions were actually preventing qualified European Americans from enrolling in these institutions. The *Bakke* US Supreme Court decision was not a favorable decision for African descendants who experienced a slowing of applications and enrollments in the nation's medical and law schools—in particular African descendant males.[8] In addition, we know that recent actions by states to eliminate Affirmative Action admission policies at the undergraduate level have resulted in significant declines in African descendant student enrollment.[9]

There has been much speculation concerning the origin and purpose of AIDS. AIDS began initially as a problem mainly for homosexual males (mainly European American males). However, before long, AIDS began to infiltrate the African descendant population through drug users who shared hypodermic needles. It wound its way into the African descendant male prison population, and ultimately became a major killer among the African descendant heterosexual population. Today, according to the US Center for Disease Control, African descendants bear "the most severe burden of HIV" (the antecedent to AIDS).[10] Whatever its origin or initial intent, AIDS has played a significant role in reducing the African descendant population and limiting the number

---

[8]Susan Welch and John Gruhl (1998), *Affirmative Action and Minority Enrollments in Medical and Law Schools*, University of Michigan Press, Ann Arbor, Michigan.
[9]Jeff Shweers (2015), "Black Enrollment at UF Takes a Hit," *Gainesville Sun*, January 31st. Retrieved from the Internet on April 14, 2015; http://www.gainesville.com/article/20150131/ARTICLES/150139930?p=1&tc=pg.
[10]See a CDC Report, "HIV in the US: *At a Glance*." (Last updated March 12, 2015). Retrieved from the Internet on April 14, 2015; http://www.cdc.gov/hiv/statistics/basics/ataglance.html.

of African descendants available to enjoy the second freedom.

It appears that the crack cocaine epidemic served as part-one of a two-part strategy to reduce the number of African descendant males who were available in the population and able to procreate. There is some evidence that the proliferation of crack cocaine in certain African descendant areas of influence was the result of decision-making by selected US government officials.[11] The highly addictive nature of crack cocaine caused users to pursue drug using by any means necessary—including criminal acts of theft and violence to obtain funds to purchase the drug. In addition, a key characteristic of the crack cocaine user was a proclivity to focus almost their entire waking state on obtaining and using the drug, which removed them from almost all economically productive activities. It turned out that the crack cocaine epidemic became one of the most adverse and disruptive forces that African descendants had ever seen: Breaking down favorable economic production, spawning crime and violence, and destroying the family structure.

The second part of the crack cocaine epidemic was the expansion of the prison industrial complex. Given the disparate nature of prison sentencing associated with crack versus powder cocaine, and the fact that African descendants were greater users of crack versus powder cocaine, African descendants males were arrested at disproportionately high rates for their association with trafficking and using crack cocaine. In addition, the thefts and violent crimes that were linked to crack cocaine use also increased the number of African descendants who were incarcerated. Consequently,

---

[11] See "The Contras, Cocaine, and Covert Operations" from the National Security Archives of The George Washington University. Retrieved from the Internet on April 14, 2015; http://nsarchive.gwu.edu/NSAEBB/NSAEBB2/nsaebb2.htm.

during the 1980s, we saw an upsurge in the number of incarcerated Africa descendants.[12] This trend continued all the way until 2009, when the US prison population began to decline slightly. Citing data from the Bureau of Justice Statistics, CBS News reported that by 2012 African descendants comprised nearly 40% of US prisoners, while only comprising about 13% of the US population.[13] Again, these African descendants, particularly males, were eliminated from the pool of those who could enjoy the second freedom. Moreover, European Americans benefitted greatly from these developments as the prison industrial complex was able to grow and thrive—producing jobs, income, and wealth to mainly European American investors.

During the second half of the 1990s, the dot.com era saw a surge in the use of computers and technology like never before in the US economy. The technology industries were dominated in overwhelming fashion by European Americans and by the advent of Asian Americans into the US economy. Not only did the dot.com era generate a tremendous number of jobs and contributed significantly to the nation's productivity growth, technology companies served as great creators of new wealth. Because African descendants were largely absent from the technology industries with respect to employment, and because we did not invest proportionately in the stock market generally, and technology companies specifically, we were excluded from the benefits brought by the expansion of the industry and the

---

[12] See the National Association for the Advancement of Colored People's (NAACP's) "Criminal Justice Fact Sheet." Retrieved from the Internet on April 14, 2015; http://www.naacp.org/pages/criminal-justice-fact-sheet.

[13] Brian Montopoli (2013), "US Prison Population Falls for Third Year," CBS News, July 25th. Retrieved from the Internet on April 14, 2015; http://www.cbsnews.com/news/us-prison-population-falls-for-third-year/.

run-up in wealth that occurred with the technology companies. Even today, US African descendants only represent 5.9% of those employed in computer manufacturing, 3.7% of those employed in software publishing, and only 7.8% of those employed as computer systems designers.[14] Contrast these percentages with the fact that we comprise over 11% of the labor force.

By the mid-2007, African descendants were the selected beneficiaries of an economy that was experiencing sustained growth and record low unemployment. By 2004, the African descendant homeownership rate had risen to an historic high of 49.1%.[15] But a rollback was about to occur. The 2008-9 global financial and economic crisis caused African descendants to see a rise in our unemployment rate to 16.0% by 2010 (18.4% for African descendant males over the age of 16 years), there was a significant loss of net worth as joblessness led to home mortgage foreclosures, and a precipitous drop in homeownership rates.[16,17] By 2014, the

---

[14] These data are for 2014 and are from the Bureau of Labor Statistics, "Employed Persons by Detailed Industry, Sex, Race, and Hispanic or Latino Ethnicity." The data are derived from the *Current Population Survey*. Retrieved from the Internet on April 15, 2015; http://www.bls.gov/cps/cpsaat18.htm.

[15] See US Census Bureau data on "Homeownership Rates by Race and Ethnicity of Householder, 1994-2012." Retrieved from the Internet on April 15, 2015; http://www.census.gov/housing/hvs/files/annual12/ann12t_22.xls.

[16] See US Bureau of Labor Statistics data on "Employment Status of the Civil Noninstitutional Population by Race, Sex, and Age." Retrieved from the Internet on April 15, 2015; http://www.bls.gov/cps/aa2011/cpsaat05.htm.

[17] CNN reported that African descendants stood to lose nearly $200 billion in net worth due to foreclosures during the Great Recession. See Tami Luhby (2010), "Housing Crisis Hits Blacks Hardest," CNN, October 19th. Retrieved from the Internet on April 17, 2015; http://www.cnn.com/2010/LIVING/10/19/inam.housing.foreclosure.money/.

African descendant homeownership rate had dropped to 43%.[18] In addition, the level of debt for African descendants rose significantly as those who were unemployed borrowed for consumption purposes and sought to retool through education; student loan debt rose to crisis proportion. In February of 2015, The *Huffington Post* reported that over 40% of African descendant families held student loan debt, compared to 28% of European American families.[19] Again, these economic developments served to exclude African descendants from enjoying the benefits of the second freedoms that were supposedly won during the 1960s.

Conclusion

In many ways, the tumultuous 1960s produced important gains and a second set of freedoms for African descendants. The legal and legislative victories promised to be transformed into economic gains. However, we saw countervailing strategies implemented in sequence, which helped rollback those freedoms and impose severe pain on African descendants. The *Bakke* decision, AIDS, the crack cocaine epidemic, the expansion of the prison industrial complex, the dot.com era, and the 2008-9 global financial and economic crisis were all bullets that pierced the heart of our opportunities to experience the benefits of hard-won freedoms.

---

[18] Robert R. Callis and Melissa Kressin (2015), "Residential Vacancies and Homeownership in the Fourth Quarter of 2014," US Census Bureau, US Department of Commerce, January 29. Retrieved from the Internet on April 15, 2015; http://www.census.gov/housing/hvs/files/currenthvspress.pdf.

[19] Jillian Berman (2015), "College Debt is Crippling Black Graduates' Ability to Gain Wealth," *Huffington Post*, February 18. Retrieved from the Internet on April 15, 2015; http://www.huffingtonpost.com/2015/02/18/student-loans-race_n_6700276.html.

Nevertheless, in 2015, we are a 45 million-strong nation within a nation. We understand that even the election of an African descendant president of these United States is insufficient to guarantee improved outcomes and better times. Many argue that, since the election of Barack Obama as president, not only have we not reached the state of a "post-racial society," but that the course has actually been reversed. Not since the era of African descendant lynching, which haunted the nation during the late 19th and up to the mid-20th century have we come to know about such indiscriminate killings of African descendant males—by members of police forces no less. Therefore we know that under these conditions there must be a dramatic change in circumstances if we are ever to enjoy true freedom and the benefits that it produces. Consequently, our minds and hearts now turn toward the formation of a new strategy that will produce such a freedom—*A 3rd Freedom.*

A 3rd Freedom

Introduction

The first freedom was joyous, but unfulfilling. The second freedom reflected an error in strategy, and the enemy devised tactics to undo the second freedom at every turn. Therefore, it is now time for African descendants to collaborate on designing a strategically sound third freedom that is guaranteed to meet our aspirations for the long term. What is the nature of this third freedom? How can it be operationalized? Which fruits will it produce? Will the eating of those fruits be satisfying and satisficing? These are the questions that we attempt to answer in this section of the monograph. It is not a *fait accompli*. Rather, it is intended as the beginning of a thought process that will, hopefully, involve many, many contributors. If we are fortunate, and if we fulfill our destiny, then we will be successful in designing and implementing this third freedom, which will meet our every needs and fulfill the desires of every heart.

Here are the issues that we intend to address in this final section. In order to ignite interest and detonate the African descendant body politic for action to achieve the third freedom, there must be recognition that this freedom should be sought. It is akin to those who are informed about the true status quo of African descendants in America informing the masses that they are naked and require clothes. After awakening to this reality, we must decide what types of "clothes" we want and how we want to obtain them. At least a partial answer to the latter questions is "reparations," which may secure for us land and a portion of the resources that are due in order to create our own world. That world could very well be our own nation; a homeland that we may call Shabazzland or whatever name we choose. What is this homeland? For all intents and purposes, it is an answer to our prayers and a solution to our problems. Of course, there is the question of whether it is appropriate to pour old wine into new skins; i.e., US African descendants who have limited experience governing ourselves being faced with the tasks of nation building, maintenance, and sustainment. We believe that there is sufficient evidence that new environments can produce new behaviors. Therefore, operationalizing this chain of realizations can produce a home for African descendants in which we can experience everlasting life.

Who told you that you were naked?

Each time a new and genuine African descendant prophet arrives on the scene and informs us that we are naked, the European American media and establishment essentially asks the question: "Who told you that you were naked?" Then they gone on to deny that we are naked and are in need of clothing. They do everything within their power to discredit the prophet. Yet an ember of this truth about our nakedness continues to smolder below the surface.

Fortunately, a lie cannot live as truth forever. In fact, the social and economic conditions that African descendants face in America compared with our European American counterparts is making it transparent that we are without sufficient clothes. It is fairly easy to find data on these conditions, so we will not present a litany of statistics to prove our point. However, it is worth pointing out a baseline reality: The average (median) European American household possesses at least 12 times more wealth than the average household that is comprised of African descendants.[20] No doubt it is true that the average (median)

---

[20] Michael Fletcher (2014), "White People Have 13 Dollars for Every Dollar Held by Black Americans," *The Washington Post*, December

income of the top 60% of African descendant households have income that constitutes about 90% of the median European American household's income.[21] The problem is that income does not translate immediately into wealth. Therefore, while the top 60% of African descendant households may be able to qualify for a home mortgage and a loan to obtain an automobile, let one of the earners in that household loose his/her job and, in a short period of time, the pain of poverty will begin to look that household in the face. European American households, with their wealth, can weather the loss of a job for an extended period—generally long enough to regain employment. Keep in mind that the bottom 40% of African descendants live below or near the poverty line. For them, life is hell on a day-to-day basis, and they are quite aware that they have no economic clothes to wear.

So you have employment. In which field? Is your income growing sufficiently to outpace inflation? The reality is that African descendants are becoming increasingly educated— with college and university degrees. But these degrees are in incorrect fields relative to growth in the US economy. In May of 2014 we completed an analysis that showed unequivocally that "Black America Doesn't Benefit from the Nation's Economic Growth."[22] It turns out that we continue to see African descendant employment growth in industries

---

12th. Retrieved from the Internet on December 12, 2014; http://www.washingtonpost.com/news/get-there/wp/2014/12/12/white-people-have-13-dollars-for-every-dollar-held-by-black-americans/.

[21] See page 2, footnote 3 of Brooks B. Robinson (2014A), "How Would US Afrodescendants Vote?" BlackEconomics.org. Retrieved from the Internet on April 20, 2015; http://www.BlackEconomics.org/BEFuture/HOWAV.pdf .

[22] Brooks B. Robinson (2014B), "Black America Doesn't Benefit from the Nation's Economic Growth," BlackEconomics.org, Honolulu, HI. Retrieved from the Internet on April 16, 2015; http://www.blackeconomics.org/BELit/BADNEG.pdf.

that have slower profit growth than the highest profit growth industries. Therefore, our employment income rises more slowly than for European Americans who are experiencing significant employment growth in the high profit growth industries. At the same time, as we discussed in Section 2 of this monograph, African descendants continue to build up high debt loads in the form of student loans to obtain a college or university education. Does it make sense to obtain an education in fields that lead to jobs that are guaranteed to pay less because they are in slow-growth or dying industries? Are we steered into these low-paying industries? Are we academically unprepared (because we attend poor-quality urban elementary and secondary schools) to train in fields that are associated with fast profit growth industries? Do we not see ourselves falling further behind in wealth accumulation because of these outcomes?

And if it were not enough that African descendants are on the losing side of the wealth gap, and that we are corralled into obtaining education in fields that ensure that we obtain low employment income relative to European Americans, is it not a worst case scenario that we are not protected physically in the American social system? Why are we experiencing the modern-day lynchings of Travon Martin, Eric Garner, Michael Brown, Tamir Rice, Walter Scott, and Freddie Gray? Why must we cry to the world that "Black Lives Matter"? African descendant males, young and old alike, are naked to the hail of bullets that snuff out our lives. We need bullet-proof clothing and there is no doubt about it. The sad fact is that, while we seek to find ways to improve our economic and social plight, the American economic system continues to favor European Americans. Think about it: So police brutality calls for body cameras that will be designed, manufactured, and merchandised by European Americans who will become enriched as a result of our suffering.

Who told you that you are naked? The above facts awaken us to this reality, and we can see for ourselves and tell ourselves that we are naked. The next important question is, what are we going to do about it?

What do African descendants want?

As history would have it, the question "What do African descendants want?" has always been improper. Why? Because there have always been multiple African descendant groups in the US. At the point of the first freedom, two primary African descendant groups existed: (1) Those who were "free" and lived in the northern and western portion of the nation; and (2) newly freed slaves who were in the southern portion of the nation. At the point of the second freedom in the 1960s, there were at least three African descendant groups: (1) Those educated and professional African descendants along with the sports and art entertainers who had relatively high levels of income and favored integration; (2) members of "radical" groups who wanted to "burn it down" and who wanted a fresh start in the US, Africa, or elsewhere; and (3) poor and uneducated African descendants who were not well-enough informed to make a wise decision concerning what was in their best interest. Today, we face an even more fractured situation. According to Eugene Robinson (2010) there are at least four groups of African descendants in America: (1) The superrich; (2) the want-to-be-rich; (3) the poor; and (4) African descendant immigrants.[23] Presumably each group has its own agenda.

From our perspective, such a fractured group creates a difficult task of identifying commonalities and a common

---

[23] Eugene Robinson (2010), *Disintegration: The Splintering of Black America*, First Anchor Books, New York, New York.

agenda on which to move forward. Without such identification, it is ridiculous to discuss the question, "What do African descendants want?" So let us sort through this splintered body.

First, the superrich think that they are sitting pretty because they have the wherewithal to purchase most things that they desire; they are, in certain cases, billionaires. Unfortunately, however, they play music to someone else's tune. Consequently, you seldom see these superrich defying the status quo and stepping out of the power structure's party line. They know that, if they do, then they will find themselves in some type of tax or legal quagmire that will suck their fleeting wealth away from them rapidly. Notice that, in most cases, a prerequisite for reaching this superrich status is to marry a European American who keeps track of developments for those who need to know. The superrich are in favor of the status quo. Even if they come to hate their condition, they will never give it up because of pride. They cannot bring themselves to contribute to a fall after rising so high. Therefore, they remain locked happily or unhappily in the superrich game.

Second, the want-to-be-rich African descendants are also on board with maintaining the status quo. They are convinced that, given enough time and luck, they can achieve superrich status. That is why we see so many African descendants bent on making it in professional sports or as a rapper. These African descendants will forego the opportunity to achieve an average life by taking on a "regular" job in lieu of struggling through poverty hoping that they will one day get a break. They do not realize that "connections" are essential to getting that break, and that they must sell their souls to participate in the superrich game.

Third, poor African descendants hate the status quo. These African descendants are like Malcolm X's "field Negroes." They want to "burn it down." They want change. They want freedom within a new order. The important difference between poor African descendants today and poor African descendants during the second freedom is that they are educated and well-informed enough to see reality clearly and to make decisions concerning what is in their best interest. Television, radio, computers, and the Internet have enabled these African descendants to know the artificiality of the superrich and want-to-be-rich game. These African descendants realize that it is insane to think that European Americans are ever going to give up their position of power and wealth. More importantly, they understand that it would be crazy for European Americans to allow African descendants to achieve a positon to do to them what they have done to us. Therefore, many among poor African descendants want out of this unfair game. They want to initiate a new game; one in which they are in charge. It is within these ranks that we find the seeds of desire for formation of an African descendant nation.

Fourth, immigrants of African descent come to America with the hope of improving their lot in life and getting rich. To aid them in this effort, some (especially those from Northern Africa) even identify themselves as white. For those that are too dark to pass for white, they distinguish themselves by their African names and their spoken accent. As you know, European Americans, like most other groups, prefer to live, work, and associate with those that look, think, act, and sound like them. Consequently, European Americans take quite naturally to many Africans who emulate well their former colonizers. At the same time, we should not minimize the effort that these African descendants undertake to make it in America. It turns out that within a generation, they produce offspring that attend some of the best colleges and universities in the country. More importantly, they are not afraid of the sciences and technology and they obtain degrees in these fields and the related jobs and income. To put it simply, while many of these African descendant immigrants claim affinity with the African descendants of former slaves, the former really hanker for life in the suburbs with European Americans and away from the poverty of urban America where many African descendants of former slaves live.

Painting this fractured picture begs the question of a need for a new or third freedom. As discussed, the superrich, the want-to-be-rich, and the immigrants are comfortable with the status quo. It appears that the only group that has a thirst for a third freedom is the poor. A priori, one might conclude that the poor are not well-positioned to ignite movement toward a third freedom. Such a conclusion is correct today. However, there can be a turn of events—and we are seeing it now—such as the senseless and cruel murders of African descendants in the streets by policemen no less, which can cause two, three, or four of the groups to coalesce and detonate a massive push toward a third freedom. When this occurs, it will become very clear what African descendants want. Yes we want access to opportunity to obtain material wealth on an even playing field basis. We want freedom from bias and racism. We want freedom from a life deck of cards that is stacked against us from the outset. We want freedom from being shot down in the back in the streets like dogs. We want to be respected for who we are the way we are. Inherently, we know that all of this freedom can only be obtained in a land of our own. Nevertheless, we should not make jazz decisions about what we want and how to go about getting it. Rather, we should develop a long-term strategic plan for the future that is systematic in its approach to identifying our needs and how we want to go about fulfilling them.

Reparations

In "The Case for Reparations," Ta-Nehesi Coates (2014) describes quite comprehensively the circumstances and conditions under which US African descendants have found ourselves historically that generate the *raison d'etre* for reparations.[24] Shortly before Coates' article was published, the Caribbean Community of Nations (CARICOM) issued its 10-Point Reparations Plan, which calls for former European colonizers to heal historical wrongs and injustices via reparations.[25] In April of 2015, the Institute of the Black World 21st Century conducted a National/International Summit on Reparations in New York City in order to jump start a reparations effort in the US for African descendants.[26] Consequently, we see a new push for reparations unfolding, which will include efforts by US African descendants to receive compensation, in some form, for the inhumane treatment and the degrading injustices that we have endured in the US for nearly 400 years. What is so surprising about this new push is that it has taken so long. In fact, Robinson (2014B) put forth the proposition that "Black Americans

---

[24] Ta-Nehesi Coates (2014), "The Case for Reparations," *The Atlantic*, June. Retrieved from the Internet on April 17, 2015; http://www.theatlantic.com/features/archive/2014/05/the-case-for-reparations/361631/.

[25] CARICOM. (2014), "CARICOM Leaders Accept Caribbean Reparatory Justice Programme as Basis for Further Action on Reparations," March 18, 2014 press release. Retrieved from the Internet on December 8, 2014, http://www.caricom.org/jsp/pressreleases/2014.jsp?menu=communications.

[26]See "Highlights of National/International Reparations Summit" (2015) from BlackEconomics.org. Retrieved from the Internet on April 17, 2015; http://www.blackeconomics.org/BEFuture/SUMHIGH.pdf.

Don't Want Reparations."[27]   But that all seems to be changing now.

As in the case of characterizing fully what African descendants want, we should be systematic in our approach and in our push for reparations; i.e., we should develop a long-term strategic plan that has reparations as just one of its components. However, assuming that reparations is placed on the anvil, there are at least two very important questions to be answered. First, for which specific circumstances, conditions, and outcomes will we seek reparations? In our view, for example, it is quite appropriate to pursue reparations that are related to economic factors. On the other hand, it is quite inappropriate and unacceptable to seek reparations for criminal factors (e.g., murder, rape, etc.). No one can ever pay us for the crimes and atrocities that were committed against our ancestors' humanity. The wounds are too deep. They should be allowed to remain open and fester in the international public eye into perpetuity. We should not allow European Americans to seek to pay us for these dastardly crimes and atrocities that were committed by their ancestors in order to close this very ugly chapter in history. It should never be closed. It should remain open forever. Our race consciousness will never allow us to forget it; they too should not be allowed to forget.

Second, what form should reparation payments take? Quite often, US African descendants have discussed colloquially receiving per capita cash reparations payments, which could be expended through individual choice. In our view, this would be a momentous mistake. Why? Mainly because, as you know, no matter the size of such payments, most of the money, as it does today, would leave our hands immediately

[27] Brooks B. Robinson (2014C), "Black Americans Don't Want Reparations," BlackEconomics.org. Retrieved from the Internet on April 17, 2015; http://www.blackeconomics.org/BELit/BADWAR.pdf.

and be returned to the hands of European Americans—further enriching them. We also do not advocate for resources being set aside in trust funds that can be used for educational purposes. As before, African descendants might use the funds to obtain education, but they may continue to be steered into educational fields that are not profitable and that lead to jobs in slow profit growth or dying industries. We have considered this question in some detail and have written on the topic (Robinson, 2015).[28] Our suggestion is that US African descendants negotiate for reparations in the form of land for nation building, material resources with which to build a nation (including technology transfer), and international support to help establish our nation in the international community.

This brings us to a simple point. Today, US African descendants can initiate a surge for a third freedom in the form of our own nation. We can build our own nation, in part, using reparation payments for our nearly 400 years of suffering in America. It has been a long and difficult road, but "further on up the road..."

A Homeland

A homeland for US African descendants could be a defining point in our long-term strategic plan. The where and how of a homeland are considered in significant detail in Chapter 3, "Point Zero Nation Formation," of *Chosen: Black America's Calling* (Robinson, 2009).[29] Of course, we are not alone in calling for African descendant nation formation:

---

[28] Brooks B. Robinson (2015), "A Broad Three-Point Reparations Program for US Afrodescendants Versus CARICOM's 10-Point Program," BlackEconomics.org, March. Retrieved from the Internet on April 17, 2015; http://www.blackeconomics.org/BELit/BTPRP.pdf.
[29] Brooks B. Robinson (2009), *Chosen: Black America's Calling*, BlackEconomics.org, Honolulu, Hawaii.

Consider that, among others, Elijah Muhammad (1965) and his subsequent followers, The Republic of New Africa (2014), and economist Robert Browne (1993) have all called for nation formation as a viable option for US African descendants to achieve the freedoms that we so richly deserve.[30]

When entertaining this potential reality, it is important to keep in mind that nation formation is not an unusual phenomenon. In fact, the trend is for more nations to evolve as opposed to nations consolidating. Since the turn of the millennium two new nations have formed with a third in the making; Timore Leste, South Sudan, and Palestine, respectively. Importantly, we should not fall victim to the assertion that people of African descent cannot govern ourselves effectively. No question about it, many African nations are experiencing a multitude of difficulties: Problems in the peaceful transfer of power, systemic corruption, sporadic economic growth, and health-related epidemics. At the same time, we see a nation, such as Rwanda, that is showing such great promise after the Great Genocide that occurred there less than three decades ago. Rwanda, especially its capital city of Kigali, is enjoying democracy in full bloom, it is considered largely free of corruption, the nation's economy is growing at a persistent and fast clip, and the country has experienced no health epidemics. Rwandans will tell you that the keys to their success are: (1) Leadership with a vision; (2) planning; and (3) no reticence to remove those who do not get the job done

---

[30] Elijah Muhammad (1965), *Message to the Blackman in America*, Secretarius MEMPS Publications, Phoenix, Arizona; BlackPast.org (2014), "Republic of New Africa (1968-)," Retrieved from the Internet on December 3, 2014, http://www.blackpast.org/aah/republic-new-africa-1968; and Robert S. Browne (1993), "The Economic Basis for Reparations to Black America," *The Review of Black Political Economy,* Vol. 21, No. 3; pp. 99-110.

after sufficient time and resources have been provided to complete a task. Granted Rwanda's population is only about 12 million. Nevertheless, it seems reasonable that US African descendants can apply some of the same strategies and principles that work in Rwanda to our population of some 45 million. Moreover, we have been very close observers of a US system that has fared quite well historically, and we can sift through that history and identify good principles for governance and economic growth.

Is a homeland the answer for US African descendants' drive for freedoms? The fact that it has been suggested historically—since the 19th century—makes it seem reasonable to give it a try. What we know is that we have been unsuccessful in living peaceable and unfettered lives in America through the course of two freedoms. Therefore, logic says that we should make another effort to achieve freedom using a different strategy. At the risk of being redundant, we must realize that European Americans will never surrender their position of power in America, and that they are too wise to allow US African descendants to reach a state where we can do to them what they have done to us. Therefore, given our high desires for life for ourselves and for our posterity, our best option may very well be to form our own new nation. Now, let us consider what that means.

PAPS (Prayers answered and problems solved)

As a US African descendant, in your heart of hearts, what do you desire, what do you hope for, and for what do you pray? Let us anticipate your answers. As discussed throughout this monograph, the basic aspiration is for fundamental freedom. Spiritually, we yearn for a place where the promise of true freedom is realized—*the ability to do what we want the way we want*. Economically, we hope for the right to work in a place that is not biased against us in order to produce goods and services with which to meet our needs. Educationally, we seek a place where education is open infinitely to our curiosity and learning; where the sciences and technology are not closed to us; and where we are prepared to do for self as opposed to just doing for others. Finally, socially, we wish for a place where safety and security are guaranteed and where our well-being is assured. Now let us project that all of these hopes can be fulfilled in a homeland for US African descendants.

This is not to say that this homeland will be a magical heaven; it promises to be a practical heaven. Because it will be a land mainly for US African descendants, racial discrimination should not abide. Science is now showing that stress caused by racism alone is detrimental to our health. This is a health problem that we should not experience in our homeland. This homeland may not produce excessive, often artificial and environmentally detrimental wealth to which we are accustomed in the US-- at least initially. However, the economy can be designed to produce to meet our needs. Is that not sufficient? We must be quick to remember that we can only eat one meal at a time, wear one garment at a time, and reside in one room at a time. Critically, in this homeland, we can implement a social system that addresses social evils, if they arise, differently—in a way that is akin to methods used by our ancestors in Africa. If we manage the nation's development properly, then we can install a truly human social system; one that, like the old African social systems, does not have jails.[31]

---

[31] History reveals that the original form of the language known as Swahili (Kiswahili) did not include a word for "jail." Rather, the word for "jail" was incorporated from Portuguese and English. Note that Swahili is a language that was derived from the original Bantu languages that were spoken in East Africa. History tells us all of Africa was ultimately populated from migrations out of East Africa.

Simply put, an African descendant homeland can become a place where most, if not all, of our current prayers are answered and all of our problems can be solved (PAPS). What more can we request? Therefore, we are warranted in desiring to establish a homeland. However, in order to achieve this outcome, we must fight for reparations for building our new nation, and we must self-detonate a powerful thrust for a third freedom in order to awaken the shout for reparations.

Old wine into new skins

Who poureth old wine into new skins? Typically, this is not the thing to do. But, at least on the surface, that is what we appear to do when we take the old US African descendant nation and transplant it into a new homeland. How can such an arrangement evolve favorably? Do we expect our old habits—ways of doing things—to prove successful in a completely new environment?   Absolutely not! Do not become anxious about this apparent mismatch. Why? For two reasons.

First, our struggle to awaken and fight for reparations and for the establishment of a homeland will be transformative. It will essentially produce a new man, woman, and child that we call US African descendants. We will come to realize that we are creditors, not debtors in this entire affair. Our ancestors gave their blood, bones, and lives for 246 years during slavery to the building of America, for which no payment was made. After the first freedom, we continued to go unpaid or underpaid during the Jim Crow era—or we

---

Consequently, we can extrapolate and conclude that original African people and their languages did not include the world "jail." See
Thomas Hinnebusch, Sara Mirza, and Adelheid Stein (1998), *Swahili: A Foundation for Speaking, Reading, and Writing*, 2nd Edition, University Press of America, Lanham, Maryland.

were lynched when we fought against such dehumanizing treatment. After the second freedom, when technology made our labor contributions less useful, we were transformed into economic production units that enabled European Americans to benefit from our suffering.[32] As we reexamine this narrative, see our legitimate right to reparations, and engage in the fight for the establishment of a homeland, we will become a renewed and proud nation of people. For this reason, old wine will not be poured into new skins.

Second, and more scientifically, it is common knowledge that, while the controversy continues over whether nature or nurture is more important in development, there is no doubt that the environment in which the nurturing occurs is a critical contributor to outcomes. In other words, just the fact that we will be in a new environment that is devoid of racial discrimination and the stress of racism will be renewing, refreshing, and energizing. We will develop pride for our nation. We will develop a strong work ethic to prove to the world that we are not "shiftless and lazy" as the former master was apt to contend. In addition, as long as our leadership designs the economic system properly, we will be motivated to work to show that we can produce for our needs

---

[32] We were production units in the sense that we became pupils that filled seats in dysfunctional and bloated educational systems; we became consumers of illegal drugs, which helped operate a subculture that thrived on guns and entertainment that were produced in the US and that spread around the globe; we became receptors of HIV AIDS, diabetes, and heart disease, which helped drive enormous growth in the medical and pharmaceutical industries; and we became prisoners that fed a beast called the prison industrial complex. In each case, the government indicated that we were a burden because of the costs associated with the production of the services that were linked to these social ills. However, while the government was often the payer, in most cases European American labor and companies were the recipients of the payment. We were the human capital units that enabled the production.

and to create wealth for our posterity. Also, given the proper social structure, and as one big family of African descendants, we will abstain from committing the type of dysfunctional social behaviors that slow the forward evolution of our society. For these reasons, too, we will not pour old wine into new skins.

On the contrary, we will pour re-aged, new wine into a new skin—our new homeland. That wine and that skin will work well together to produce a nation that has the potential to serve as a very positive influence on the entire world. We were the best that Africa had to offer the European. We were cast downward. But the arising of our new homeland will show the world that the last can be first. In the end, our arising shall be sufficient to lead the way for African descendants around the world to arise above the inhumanity and excessive materialism (which is mainly what the European has brought to the world stage) in order to produce a world of harmony and peace.

Everlasting life

In the spirit and physical realms, it may be possible to experience everlasting life. If we perpetually transplant souls (the essential life force) from dying bodies into living ones, then we can achieve this outcome. This is an old African practice that we must re-perfect. However, this is not the type of everlasting life about which we want to focus here. Our attention is on a pragmatic everlasting life. Specifically, we are referring to a space and time, which we can enjoy in a homeland where we cherish each other. The fulfillment of such a notion is embodied in our preservation of each life. Recall the *griot*? In the African tradition, an oral historian records the lives of each member of the village into perpetuity. Given today's technology, we don't need a *griot*, just a willingness to cherish each other and to retain a record of each other's lives.

In the US, our lives are not valued. Each one of us represents just a statistic for European Americans, and just another life that did not produce freedom for our fellow African descendants. But when we realize a homeland, our new freedom, renewed faith, and elevated care and love for each other will cause us to want to record each African descendant's contributions to the development and evolution of the nation. Our museums will do their jobs. Families, too, with more resources made possible by the nation, will take the time and care to preserve a record of (immortalize) our lives.

In just a few hundred years—and the world will extend through this period because of our contributions to world progress—it will be common to find families within our homeland that can call forth the names and lives of 24 generations. It will be in that day that the great breakthrough may occur and we will finally discern the true meaning of life itself. Lo and behold it will have all been made possible by our thirst for, and willingness to fight for, *A 3rd Freedom*.

Epilogue

For US African descendants, there can be no peace without a third freedom and the realization of a homeland. There can be no homeland without reparations. For European Americans, there can be no peace vis-à-vis US African descendants without the dispensing of reparations. In the context of the eight stage process of reconciliation and atonement, European Americans must become Godly sorrowful for the historical transgressions that they and their forefathers have committed against humanity and they must fulfill stage five of the process. That is, they must atone, which is operationalized through reparations. The longer that both sides delay fulfilling these requirements for peace the more difficult they will become to fulfill.

Let us hope that the road to reparations and a homeland does not go through violent conflict. However, nothing of value is ever surrendered easily. Our forefathers have died in the struggle for freedom. Do we place ourselves above their fate? Let us be clear, the freedom that we seek is for future generations. Let us fight now to claim that freedom on their behalf. What will they say if we fail to do this?

US African descendants have endured two unfulfilling and unsatisfying freedoms: (1) The Emancipation Proclamation and the Civil War freeing of slaves; and (2) the Civil Rights era freedoms. There are three primary reasons why these two freedoms turned out to be busts for African descendants. First, European Americans only agreed to the paper notions of these freedoms, and did not become Godly sorrowful for the wrongs that had been wrought. Second, the wrong parties were placed in charge of enforcing the freedoms that had been won. Third, sufficient resources were never appointed to enforce the freedoms. This failure to repent, takes seriously the administration of these freedoms, and allocate resources to enforcing these freedoms proved to be successful only in delaying the day when justice must be served.

The day of justice is drawing near. Today, US African descendants are joining with African descendants in the Caribbean to issue a call for reparations. Before too long, people of African descent throughout the Western Hemisphere and across Africa will issue a shout for atonement in the form of reparations. All we have to do is to remain committed to the cause and not allow Europeans to use the age old divide-and-conquer-schemes (tricknology) that they have used in the past to disable our march toward freedom.

Freedoms one and two may have failed, but this third freedom that is just up the road promises to enable us to be free indeed. Call it fate. Call it chance. Call it luck. The third freedom will be a charmed freedom—the one that will be solid and true. It will not come magically. We must fight for it. It is a freedom for which we have longed. It is a freedom that we desire greatly, and which we so richly deserve. It is a freedom that we must have. Now, let us reach out together and take it!

Index

10-Point Reparations Plan, *25*

Abernathy
  Ralph, *16*
abolitionist movement, *13*
ACS, *8*
Affirmative Action, *5*, *13*, *14*, *16*, *17*
AIDS, *6*, *16*, *17*, *19*, *29*
American Colonization Society
  ACS, *8*
ancestors, *25*, *28*

Bakke, *5*, *16*, *17*, *19*
bellum
  post, *8*, *10*, *11*, *12*
Berman
  Jillian, *19*
Black towns, *9*, *11*, *12*
Brown
  Michael, *22*
Brown vs. Board of Education, *13*
Browne
  Robert, *26*
bullets, *19*, *22*
Bureau of Justice Statistics, *18*
Bureau of Labor Statistics, *18*, *19*
Burin
  Eric, *8*
burn it down, *23*

Callis
  Robert, *19*
Caribbean Community of Nations
  CARICOM, *25*
CARICOM
  Caribbean Community of Nations, *25*, *26*
CBS News, *18*
Census Bureau, *19*
Center for Disease Control, *17*
Chiriqui Plan, *8*
Civil Rights Act, *5*, *13*
Civil War, *5*, *7*, *8*, *9*, *12*, *31*
CNN, *19*
Coates
  Ta-Nehesi, *24*, *25*
computers, *18*, *23*
consolidation, *11*, *12*
consumption, *19*
crack cocaine, *6*, *16*, *17*, *18*, *19*

debt, *19*, *22*
desegregation, *13*, *14*, *15*, *16*
discrimination, *17*, *27*, *29*
dot.com era, *16*, *18*, *19*
DuBois
  W.E.B., *9*

economic, *5*, *6*, *7*, *11*, *14*, *16*, *17*, *19*, *21*, *22*, *25*, *27*, *28*, *29*

Emancipation Proclamation, *7, 9, 12, 31*
employment, *14, 16, 18, 21, 22*
environment, *10, 28, 29*
epidemics, *27*
Executive Order, *13, 14*

Fair Housing Act, *5, 13*
families, *7, 14, 19, 30*
Fletcher
   Michael, *21*
Florida, *8, 11*
Freedom Rides, *13*

Garner
   Eric, *22*
George Washington
   University, *17*
Georgia, *5, 10*
Gray
   Freddie, *22*
Great Genocide, *27*
Great Recession, *6, 16, 19*
griot, *29*
growth, *10, 11, 18, 21, 26, 27, 29*
Gruhl
   John, *17*

Hamilton
   Kenneth, *9*
health, *27, 28*
Higgs
   Robert, *5, 9, 10, 11*
Hinnebusch
   Thomas, *28*
HIV, *6, 17, 29*

homeownership, *18*
Homestead Act, *9*
household, *21*
Huffington Post, *19*
human capital, *10*

immigrants, *23, 24*
income, *6, 18, 21, 22, 24*
independent living
   arrangements, *7, 8, 9, 10, 11*
Indian Territory, *9*
inhumane, *25*
Institute of the Black, *25*
integration, *11, 13, 14, 15, 16, 22*

jail, *28*
Jim Crow, *5, 6, 12, 16, 28*
jobs, *18, 22, 24, 26, 30*
Johnson
   Lyndon, *13, 14, 16*

Kigali, *27*
King
   Martin Luther, Jr., *5, 16*
Kressin
   Melissa, *19*

labor force, *18*
land, *5, 7, 8, 9, 12, 20, 24, 26, 27*
Liberia, *8*
Lincoln
   Abraham, *8, 9*
Lunch Counter Sit-Ins, *13*
Lusane
   Clarence, *8*

49

lynching, *20*

March on Washington, *5, 13*
Martin
  Travon, *5, 22*
median, *21*
Mirza
  Sara, *28*
money, *11, 16, 19, 26*
Montgomery Bus Boycott,
  5, 13
Montopoli
  Brian, *18*
Muhammad
  Elijah, *26*

NAACP, *18*
naked, *20, 21, 22*
nation, *6, 7, 9, 11, 14, 17,*
  18, 19, 20, 22, 24, 26, 27,
  28, 29, 30
nation building, *11, 21, 26*
nation formation, *7, 9, 26*
North Carolina
  Wilmington, *11*
Northwest Ordinance, *9*
Northwest Territory, *7, 9*

Obama
  Barack, *6, 19*
Oklahoma, *9, 11*

Palestine, *27*
police, *6, 20, 22*
poor, *22, 23, 24*
population, *7, 11, 12, 14,*
  15, 17, 18, 27
post-racial, *20*

prison industrial complex, *6,*
  16, 18, 19, 29

racism, *24, 28, 29*
radio, *23*
reparations, *20, 25, 28, 31*
Republic of New Africa, *26*
resources, 7, 9, 13, 15, 20,
  26, 27, 30
Rice
  Tamir, *22*
Robinson
  Brooks B., *ii, 11, 21, 22,*
    25, 26
  Eugene, 23
Rosewood
  Florida, *11*
Rwanda, *27*

Science, *28*
Scott
  Walter, *22*
Selma March, *13*
Shabazzland, *20*
Shweers
  Jeff, *17*
South Sudan, *26*
Stein
  Adelheid, *28*
stock market, *18*
Summit, *25*
superrich, *23, 24*
Swahili, *28*

Taylor
  Quintard, *9*
technology, *6, 18, 24, 26,*
  27, 28, 30

Television, *23*
Till
    Emmitt, *12*
Timore Leste, *26*
tricknology, *31*
Tulsa
    Oklahoma, *11*

unemployment, *6*, *18*
unfair game, *24*

Vagrancy Laws, *12*

want-to-be-rich, *23*, *24*
wealth, *6*, *10*, *11*, *12*, *18*, *21*,
    22, *23*, *24*, *28*, *29*
Welch
    Susan, *17*
Wilmington
    North Carolina, *11*

Other publications from Dr. Brooks B. Robinson and BlackEconomics.org.

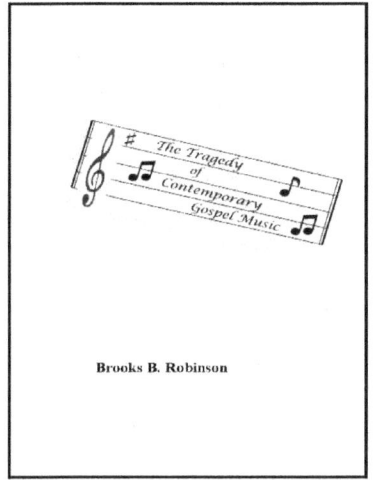

The Tragedy of Contemporary Gospel Music (2014). A monograph that analyzes the extent to which Afrodescendants use tools at our disposal to solve our problems.

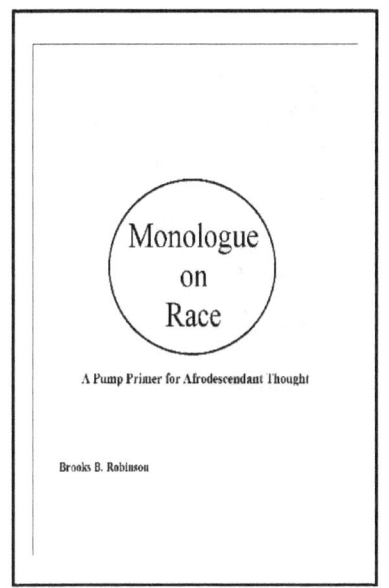

Monologue on Race (2013). Invites Black Americans to consider today's status quo and appropriate responses to it. It is a 360-degree thinking guide on Afrodescendant issues.

Pay to Let Us Go*:
**Afrodescendants'
Benefits and Costs
to America*** (2012).
Explores the fiscal
burden that Blacks
impose on the
American society.
We estimate the
benefits and costs,
and compute the
burden.

53 (2011). A
monograph that
recounts
Afrodescendants'
nation formation
efforts, and
provides a
statistical analysis
of seven socio-
economic
categories in a
"53" paradigm out
to 2050.

A Trilogy:

Change: Black America's Religion (2010) A book that presses Black America to develop a religion "for us by us," which will enable successful and prosperous nation formation.

Chosen: Black America's Calling (2009) A book that enables Black Americans to identify our proper role for the current millennium, to recognize the need for movement, and to formulate a realistic strategy for nation formation.

Choice: Black America's Decision (2009). A futuristic social essay that transmits the seed of nation formation for Black America.

Source Book

BlackEconomics: A Primer (2007). A ready reference on Black economics. It contains 54 entries on economic concepts and terms, on Black personalities, and on Black socioeconomic conditions and institutions.

www.ingramcontent.com/pod-product-compliance
Lightning Source LLC
Chambersburg PA
CBHW070821290526
45795CB00002B/801